Amazing Questions & Answers

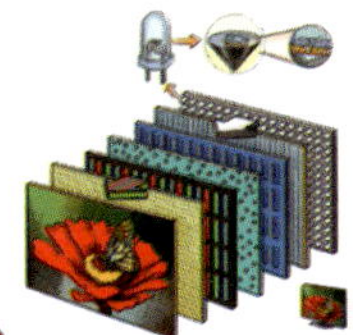

Inventions

Om Books International

Om Books International

Reprinted in 2024

Corporate & Editorial Office
A-12, Sector 64, Noida 201 301
Uttar Pradesh, India
Phone: +91 120 477 4100
Email: editorial@ombooks.com
Website: www.ombooksinternational.com

Sales Office
107, Ansari Road, Darya Ganj
New Delhi 110 002, India
Phone: +91 11 4000 9000
Email: sales@ombooks.com
Website: www.ombooks.com

ISBN: 978-93-52763-03-0

Printed in India

10 9 8 7 6 5

How?

How was fire discovered?

What?

When can I see the Orionids?

What is a smart watch?

When?

Why?

Why were stickers invented?

CONTENTS

$1
$

How?

How old is the oldest invention?

It's as old as around 3 million years! The oldest inventions are said to be the most basic stone implements that were made by early humans. These include stone cores, hammer-stones, anvils and sharp stone flakes. These tools were made by hitting stones against each other, or applying pressure with wood or bones. Early men used these tools for hunting and protecting themselves.

> **Pocket fact**
>
> **The oldest tools!**
> The world's oldest stone tools were discovered from the shores of Lake Turkana in Kenya, and are almost 3 million years old!

> **Find out**
>
> How did the ancient Greeks light a fire?

How was fire discovered?

There are several theories on how fire was discovered. Some believe that pre-humans first noticed fire after lightning struck a tree. It is said that then they must have learnt to make fire using sticks and flint. Soon, they discovered that it was possible to use fire for heat, light and cooking food.

How were wheels used in ancient times?

They first served as a potter's wheel! Wheels first appeared in Mesopotamia more than 5,000 years ago. They were initially used by potters for shaping clay. It was much later that wheels were fitted to carts, which made movement much easier.

Try this!

Name the parts of a wheel.

Pocket fact

No wheels exist in nature!
Throughout history, most inventions were inspired by the natural world. The idea to invent fork came from forked sticks; the airplane from gliding birds. But the wheel was not inspired by any existing object; it was purely man's innovation.

How is a crossbar similar to the modern wheel?

It had spokes and a crossbar! The crossbar was invented after the early semi-solid wheels. It had a piece of wood called crossbar running from one side of the wheel to the other to make it stronger. It also had spokes that linked the middle of the wheel to the outer edge. It looked similar to the modern wheel, especially the wheel of a bicycle.

How old are the first writing records?

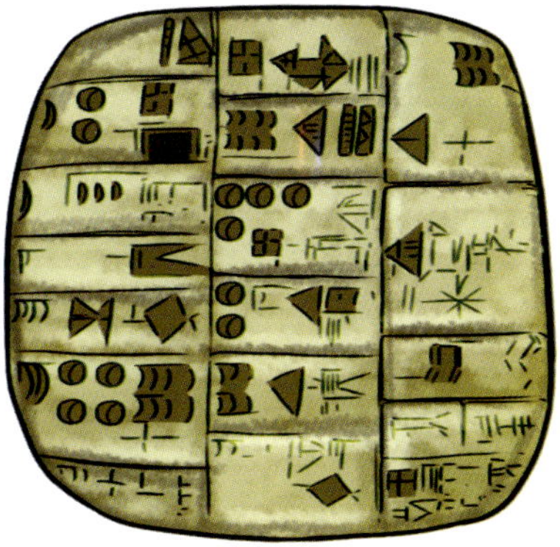

Approximately 5,000 years old! The earliest writing we know of, dates back to around 3,000 BCE and was probably invented by the Sumerians, who lived in southern Mesopotamia. However, it was much different from the present-day writing. Most early writing systems began with symbols and small images instead of words.

Pocket fact

Quill pen!
The quill, the hollow shaft of a bird's feather, was also used as a writing tool in the ancient times. It was first used as a pen in around 500 CE.

Find out

When did the alphabet first originate?

How did the first writing tool look?

It was a pointed tool! The Sumerians are credited with the invention of the first writing tool called a 'stylus'. It was made from reed, a strong thin plant, and produced a wedge shape each time it was pressed into wet clay.

How was ink made in ancient times?

It was made of carbon! The first writing ink was invented by the Egyptians and the Chinese in 2500 BCE. It was made of carbon mixed with a solution of glue or gum and moulded into sticks. The sticks were dried but they were mixed with water before use.

Pocket fact

Not blurred anymore!
Johannes Gutenberg invented a special oil-based ink in the 1400s. This ink prevented blurry edges and adhered to Gutenberg's newly invented printing press.

Find out

What has the word "paper" been derived from?

How was paper first made?

It was made from mulberry bark! Papermaking dates back to about 105 CE, when Ts'ai Lun, an official attached to the Imperial court of China made a sheet of paper using mulberry fibres. He made it by mixing mulberry bark and other fibres with old rags, hemp waste and fishnets. He then mashed it flat, pressed out the water and let it dry in the sun.

How were calculations done in the ancient times?

It started with fingers and other objects! The first method of calculation was counting on fingers. This gradually changed to the use of tallies that were made by carving notches in wood, bone and stone. Much later, around 1387 CE, the first calculating tool called the abacus was used in Europe, China and Russia.

Pocket fact

Heaven beads!

The Chinese abacus called the Suanpan had two beads on the rods on the upper side and five beads on the rods on the lower side of the divider. The upper beads are called the heaven beads and the lower beads are called the earth beads.

Try this!

Calculate 1010010 + 1001011 with the help of a calculator. Which number did you get?

How was the first mechanical calculator invented?

It was invented using metal wheel dials! The first mechanical calculator was invented in 1642 by Blaise Pascal. It had a polished brass box, about 350 mm x 125 mm x 75 mm in dimension. There were eight movable metal dials with the numbers 0-9 that were turned to the appropriate numbers using a stylus. The answers were displayed in boxes on the top of the calculator.

How were long-distance messages sent before the invention of the telephone?

They were sent using telegraphs. The telegraph was first invented in 1791 by Claude and Rene Chappe in France. It used sound along with times on a clock face for sending messages. But it wasn't very successful. Later, in 1837, Samuel Morse developed the electric telegraph that worked by transmitting electrical signals over a wire laid between stations.

Pocket fact

The First Message!
The first ever message over the telegraph was sent on 24 May 1844 by Morse. It was a passage from the Bible's Book of Numbers and read "What hath God wrought!"

Try this!

Take two tin cans and a string, and make a telephone with the help of your parents. When done, place a can against your friend's ear while you talk directly into the other can. Can you hear each other?

How did the Box Telephone work?

The Box Telephone was invented by Alexander Graham Bell in 1876–1877. It was made of a wooden frame that had two electromagnets, wire terminals, a horseshoe magnet and a trumpet-shaped receiver. The receiver worked as, both, a mouthpiece and an earpiece. When someone spoke into the mouthpiece, it made the electromagnets vibrate. These vibrations turned into electric signals which were taken from and sent to another telephone by wires attached on the two terminals.

How was electricity discovered?

Electricity is a form of energy which occurs naturally. It is said to have been discovered in 1752 by Benjamin Franklin. He conducted an experiment in order to show that lightning was electricity. He tied a metal key to a kite string and flew it during a thunderstorm to conduct electricity. Electricity from the storm clouds transferred to the metal key and flowed down the string!

Try this!

Be an energy saver! Every day, practice at least five ways to save electricity at home and school.

Pocket fact

The first power plant!
The first power plant, Pearl Street Power Station, built by Thomas Edison became operative in the year 1882.

How did the first electric light look?

It looked quite similar to a lantern! The first electric light was made in 1800 by an English scientist Humphry Davy. He attached a charcoal strip between the ends of two wires and connected the other ends of the wires to a battery. This charged the charcoal strip and made the carbon glow. Thus, the first arc lamp was invented.

They were much-like present-day wagons! Railways existed long before the invention of the steam engine. They were used in European mines to move heavy wagonloads of coal along tunnels. The wagons first ran on parallel wooden planks and then on iron rails. They were pulled by horses or people.

Find out

At what altitude does an airplane fly?

Pocket fact

Sorry for the delay!
In Japan, any train delays, over 5 minutes, usually incur an apology and a "delay certificate" for the passengers on their way to work.

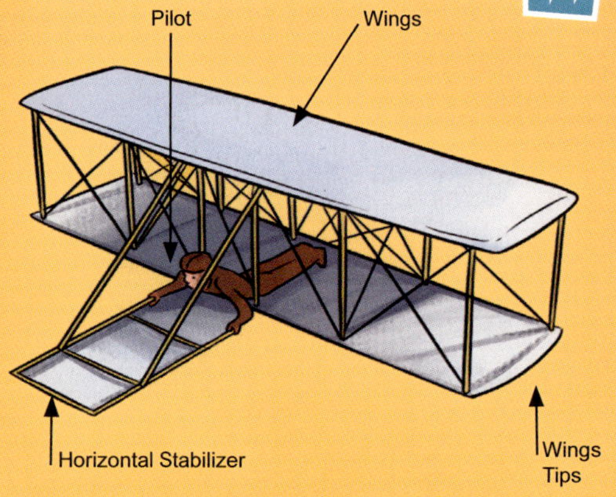

How was the first airplane different from modern airplanes?

It had many differences! The first airplane was invented by the Wright brothers in 1903. It was made of wood or canvas materials and had warped light-weight wings. Its elevators were located on the front of the aircraft. On the other hand, modern airplanes are made of aluminium. They have ailerons on their wings to control the roll of the aircraft. Their elevators are located at the tail-end of the aircraft. Modern airplanes have a cockpit with high technological controls that the first airplane lacked.

How did the early televisions work?

They displayed only black and white pictures! The first television was invented by Scottish inventor John Logie Baird. Later a Russian- American inventor Vladimir Zworykin used the cathode-ray tube (a device used to show images on a screen) in a new type of electrical television. Early televisions had huge boxes and much smaller screens. They only showed black and white pictures.

Pocket fact

I coined it!
The word "television" was introduced in the English language in 1907. It was coined by the Russian scientist, Constantin Perskyi.

Find out

What is the full form of LED?

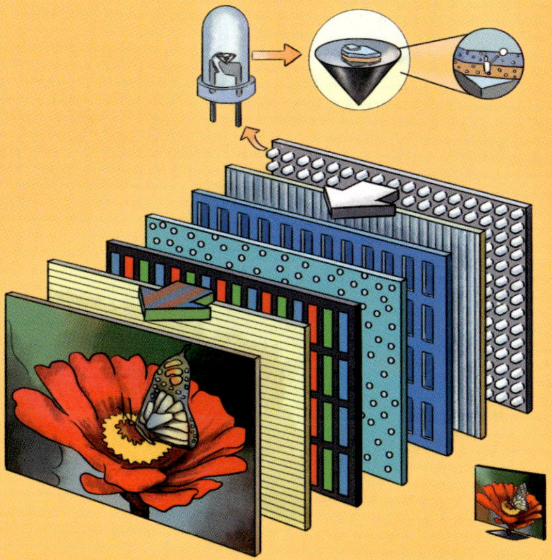

How are LED televisions different from cathode-ray tube televisions?

They used LEDs to display images! LED televisions have small LEDs behind the screen that produce high-quality images with vibrant colours. Due to the use of LEDs, the screen is power efficient and much slimmer in size. On the other hand, cathode-ray tube TVs have a cathode-ray tube that displays the image on the screen. They are large in size and have wide viewing angles.

How did the first computer look?

It was huge and complicated! The Analytical Engine is generally considered the first computer. It was invented by Charles Babbage in the early 19th century. It had four main parts that are the essential components of every computer today. The mill was the calculating unit (CPU in a modern computer), the store was where data were held prior to processing (memory in a modern computer) and the reader and printer were the input and output devices.

Try it!

Compare the keys of a typewriter and a keyboard. List the differences.

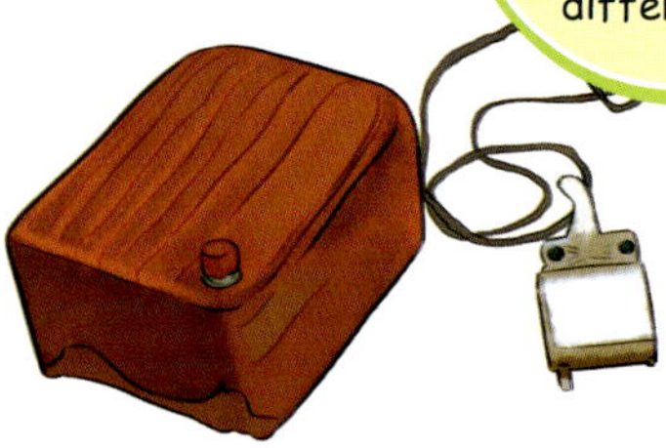

Pocket fact

ENIAC!
The first electronic computer was called the ENIAC. It weighed more than 27 tons and measured 1800 square feet.

How was the first typewriter different from the modern one?

It typed only in capital letters! The first typewriter called the Sholes and Glidden was invented by Christopher Latham Sholes. This typewriter typed only in capital letters. Its keyboard was designed to separate frequently-used pairs of type-bars so that they would not clash and get stuck at the printing point. It was a decorative machine with painted flowers and decals, and looked much like a sewing machine!

How did the idea of QWERTY keyboard evolve?

It was invented due to the keys getting jammed! The QWERTY arrangement on a keyboard was designed in 1868 by Christopher Sholes, the inventor of the typewriter. The first keyboard had keys arranged in an alphabetical order, but people typed so fast that the keys got jammed. To solve this, the keys were randomly positioned so that it could slow down the typing speed and prevent key jams.

Find out

What is the use of the pause key on the keyboard?

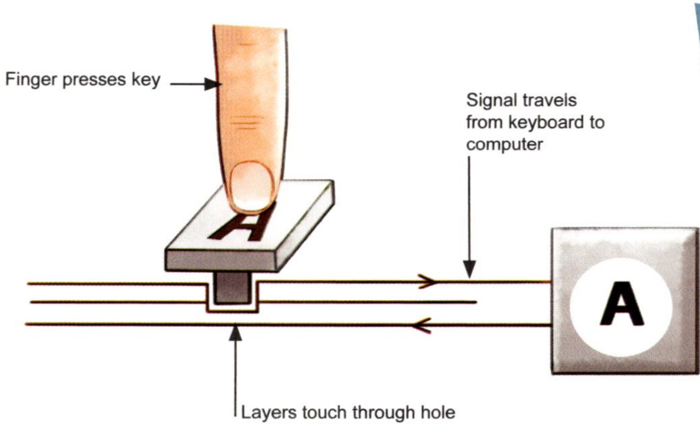

Pocket fact

Shortest in Japan!
The longest key on every keyboard is the spacebar. But in Japan, the statistical spacebar is much shorter than anywhere else in the world.

How does the keyboard put words on your screen?

It works with the help of mechanical switches! The keyboard contains its own internal processor that receives electrical signals through key strokes. Each key has a special shaped arrangement at the bottom, known as the plunger. When you press a key, an electrical signal is sent to the keyboard's internal processor. The key which is pressed is detected and letter is typed on the screen!

How did the first telescope look?

It was a simple arrangement of lenses! The first telescope was invented in 1608 by a Dutch spectacle-maker Hans Lippershey. He fitted two small lenses in a long tube. This is how the first telescope was made. In 1609, Galileo Galilei improved this telescope. Galileo's telescope was only about 47 inches long. It had an eyepiece that provided an upright image.

Pocket fact

Look and see!
The word telescope was derived from the Greek words 'tele' and 'scope,' meaning 'far' and 'to look and see'.

Find out

What is the length of a space shuttle?

How did the first space shuttle launch and land?

It launched like a rocket but landed like a glider airplane! The space shuttle was launched by NASA. It had solid rocket boosters and main engines (on the orbiter) that helped the shuttle blast off from Earth like a rocket. The two boosters dropped off the shuttle 2 minutes after the launch and fell into the ocean. The shuttle orbiter returned to Earth like an airplane, with wheels coming out from underneath its orbiter. It rolled to a stop on a runway.

How did the compass come into being?

Find out

What was GPS earlier called?

It was inspired from the fortune tellers! The compass was invented by the Chinese. Chinese fortune tellers used a mineral called lodestone to construct their fortune-telling boards. The mineral consisted of an iron oxide which aligns itself in a north-south direction. Eventually, it was noticed that the lodestones pointed out real directions. This led to the creation of the first compass. It was made on a square slab, a lodestone spoon-shaped device that would always point south.

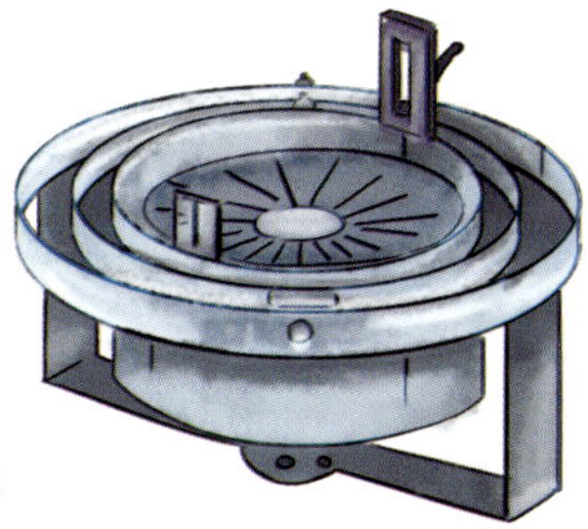

Pocket fact

That's like a tadpole!
The first needle of an iron needle compass was invented in China. It was shaped like a tadpole.

How old is the GPS system?

It started in 1957! The idea of GPS started with the satellite Sputnik. US scientists working at MIT noticed that the frequency of the radio signals transmitted by the Russian satellite Sputnik increased as it approached and decreased as it moved away. This gave them the idea to track satellites from the ground by measuring the frequency of the radio signals they emitted. This could also be used to track the location of receivers on the ground from the satellites.

What?
$1
$
e-mail
2
e-mail

What is an invention?

An invention is usually considered to be the embodiment of a new idea in the form of a device or a process that aims at solving a specific problem. It also needs to be proven workable. If the invention is new, it can be patented, making its commercial use easier and profitable.

Find out

If two people invent something together, who gets the patent?

Pocket fact

It's mine!
When someone invents something, it needs to be patented. A patent is a right that lies with the owner of an invention. It prevents others from copying, using, selling or importing the invention without his permission.

What does an inventor do?

An inventor identifies problems and concentrates on ways to solve those problems. Inventors formulate ideas, methods and processes and often design technical devices which usually make life better for human beings.

What was the first wheel made of?

The first wheel was probably made of wood. Archaeological evidences suggest that the wheel was first used in Mesopotamia, for pottery. The oldest wooden wheel discovered was found in Ljubljana, Slovenia and is believed to date back to around 3200 BCE. Wheels started being used for transportation much later.

Pocket fact

First modern bicycle!
John Kemp Starley, an English inventor and industrialist, invented the first modern bicycle in 1885.

Find out

When was the unicycle invented?

What was the first bicycle called?

The Dandy Horse! The first human means of transport that used only two wheels in tandem, was invented by the German inventor Baron Karl von Drais. It was made of a wooden frame supported by two in-line wheels. The rider sat on the wooden frame with one leg on each side and pushed the vehicle with his or her feet while steering the front wheel.
The Dandy Horse was introduced to the public in Mannheim, in 1817 and in Paris in 1818. Also called Draisine or Laufmaschine, this vehicle was the forerunner of the modern bicycle.

What was the first car like?

It was a two-seater vehicle with a four-stroke engine! The first car was invented by Carl Benz in 1885. The main features of this two-seater vehicle included—its high-speed four-stroke engine installed horizontally at the rear, the tubular steel frame, three wire-spoked wheels and the differential. It also had a controlled exhaust valve, an automatic intake slide, water/thermo siphon evaporation cooling and high-voltage electrical vibrator ignition with spark plug.

Pocket fact

30,000 parts!
A car has about 30,000 parts, counting every part down to the smallest screws. Some of these parts are made by the car manufacturing company while some are made by other suppliers.

Find out

Why do tyres have valve caps?

What is a tyre made of?

A tyre is a covering for a wheel and it is usually made of rubber. It is ring shaped and covers the rim of a wheel. Tyres used to be solid, but now only inflated tyres are used because they provide a cushioning for the wheel, to absorb shocks, when moving over rough terrains.

What does T in a T-shirt stand for?

The T in a T-shirt is usually attributed to the T-shape of the garment when laid out. This theory is also supported by the existence of A-shirts (which are also called tank tops). T-shirt is also often seen as the abbreviation for Training Shirt.

Find out

Why do shirts have collars?

Pocket fact

The first neck tie!
The necktie first originated in the 17th century in France. King Louis XIII hired Croatian mercenaries, during a war, who wore a piece of cloth called Cravat around their neck as part of their uniform.

What was the earliest clothing made of?

Animal skins! Humans have been wearing clothes since hundreds of thousands of years. The earliest clothing was probably made of animal skin. It is assumed that humans have been wearing clothes since the last part of the ice age because it would have been impossible to survive without clothing at that point.

What did people use to keep track of time, before clocks?

Objects in the sky and some devices! The first mechanical clocks started appearing in the 13th and 14th centuries. Until then, people kept track of time by looking at the sun, stars and the seasons of the year. Eventually, devices such as the sundial, obelisk, hourglass, clypsendra (based on the controlled flow of a liquid), candle clock and incense clock were invented, to keep track of time.

Pocket fact

The oldest clock!
The oldest clock in the world is located in Salisbury, England. It was created in 1386.

Find out

Why does every new clock show the time 10:10?

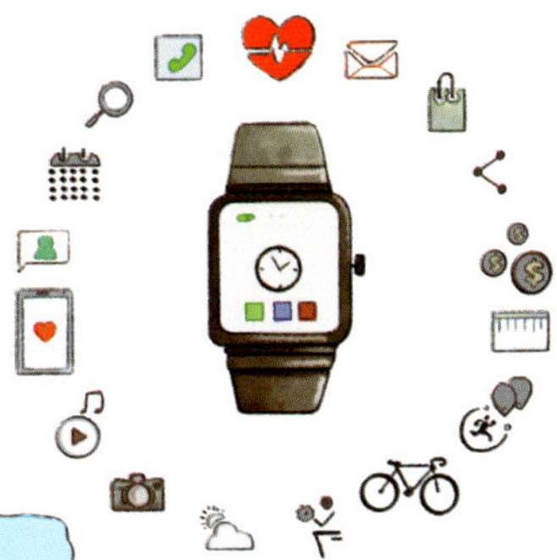

What is a smart watch?

A smart watch is a device that is equipped to do much more than just tell the time. The scope of functions for a smart watch depends on the variety that is used, but they are usually most effective when synced to a smart phone. Smart watches can do a lot but they cannot be as good as smartphones.

What is the history of shoes?

It dates backs to 1600-1200 BCE! Shoes have been used to shield the feet since ages. The earliest shoes were soft, made from wraparound leather, and resembled either sandals or moccasins. Then came rock sandals, leather shoes and sandals. In the 18th century, fabric shoes like the silk pair were considered very fashionable.

Pocket fact

No left or right!
Breaking in a new pair of shoes was not as easy as it is today. The earliest shoes were made on absolutely straight lasts. There was no difference between the right and the left shoe until 1850.

What is an aglet used for?

To keep the fibre of the shoelace from unravelling! An aglet is the hard metal or plastic coating present at the end of the shoelace, to prevent the fabric of the shoestrings from getting frayed. It also helps in putting the shoelaces through the eyelets of the shoes. Today, most of the aglets are made by wrapping the end of the shoelaces with plastic coating.

What was the first chocolate like?

It was a beverage made from the cacao bean! Chocolate history begins in Mesoamerica in 1900 BCE. The Maya, Toltec, and Aztec people cultivated the cacao tree more than 3000 years ago. However, the first people to use chocolate as a beverage were probably the Olmec of, what is today, southeast Mexico. The Maya also used chocolate in religious rituals but it was strictly for drinking purposes. Chocolate came to be used in solid form only in the 1850s.

Find out

When was the ice cream cone invented and by whom?

Pocket fact

The first chocolate bar!
The first chocolate bar was made in 1842 by the British chocolate company Cadbury.

What were the ingredients of the first ice cream?

Just ice and honey or fruits! There is no specific record of when or who invented ice cream but this cold dessert has been known to date back to the 2nd Century BCE. We know that Alexander the Great enjoyed having snow or ice flavoured with honey. Also, during the Roman Empire, Nero Claudius Caesar (CE 54–86) was known to send runners to fetch snow from the mountains so that he could have them with fruits and juices.

What is the difference between tomato sauce and tomato ketchup?

The difference between tomato sauce and tomato ketchup lies in its preparation! In the United States, tomatoes, sugar, vinegar and spices are used to make ketchup and as a rule, it is always served cold. Sauces involve the use of tomatoes, oil, meat or vegetable and spices. Vinegar is not used. Also, sauces are generally served hot.

Find out

In which year was iced tea invented and by whom?

Pocket fact

Upside-down bottle!

Ketchup bottles were not always upside down. A shop owner named Paul Brown in Mich designed a new storable upside down bottle so that it could open easily when squeezed and shut securely. It earned Paul Brown $13 million.

What is the history of tea?

The history of tea dates back to around 2700 BCE in China. Most sources also trace the origin of the tea plant to Tibet and northern India. Tea was used as a medicinal beverage for a million years. It was obtained by boiling fresh leaves in water. The popularity of tea grew around the 3rd century CE when tea cultivation and processing began and it soon became a daily drink.

What was used before notes and coins were invented?

The barter system! The medium of exchange before the invention of currency was barter, a system where transaction took place through the exchange of goods and services. It was slow and inconvenient because people had to find other people with whom they could make deals where both parties were satisfied. The barter system was slowly made easier by exchange of easily tradable goods like salt, weapons and animal skins.

> **Pocket fact**
>
> **Piggy bank!**
> The terms 'piggy bank' was derived from the word 'pygg'. In Old English, pygg was a type of clay that was used to make jars and dishes that held money.

> **Find out**
>
> How many parts does a coin have? Can you name them?

What led to the invention of the dollar sign?

The origin of the dollar sign is shrouded in mystery but the most commonly accepted theory that comes from the Bureau of Engraving and Printing is that the Spanish Peso, which was the basic currency of Spanish America, was abbreviated as PS. It is believed that the two letters merged together to lead to the formation of the US dollar sign. The sign first appeared in the 1800s and was already widely used by the time the American paper dollar was printed in 1875.

What is the history of Sudoku?

The name comes from Japan but the puzzle comes from Switzerland! Sudoku has its roots in ancient magic squares or number puzzles. In 1783, a Swiss mathematician named Leonhard Euler, devised "Latin Squares" and called it "a new kind of magic squares". It was a grid in which each number was repeated only once in each row or column. The modern Sudoku was first introduced by Howard Garnes in the American Dell magazine, New York in 1979. The difference was that the grids were subdivided into blocks of nine of 3x3 squares.

Find out

What is the meaning of the word Sudoku?

Pocket fact

Who gave the term robot?

The word "robot" was first used by Czech playwright Karel Capek in his play RUR, Rossum's Universal Robots in 1921. The play was about the destruction of humanity by robots.

What is the smallest Robot called?

It's called the RoboBee! The world's smallest robot was developed by a research team at Harvard University in 2009. RoboBee was modelled on an insect and is the smallest man-made device with a wingspan of 3-centimetres. The RoboBee project was launched to make a fully autonomous swarm of flying robots for applications such as search and rescue and artificial pollination.

E-mail ID is just another name for e-mail address. Electronic mail (e-mail) is a method of exchanging messages between people using the electronic medium. E-mails can operate across computer networks, that is, the Internet. To send and receive emails, you should have an e-mail ID. It's just like your address in a locality. The default format of an e-mail ID is Username@domain.com. You can modify the part before the @ sign. But the domain name cannot be modified.

Pocket fact

E-mail from space!
E-mails can not only travel around the world but theye-can also be sent from space. The first e-mail from space was sent in 1991 by the crew of STS-43 Atlantis. They used Apple's AppleLink software on a Macintosh Portable to send an e-mail.

Find out

The @ sign is commonly known as "at" sign or symbol. What is it actually called?

How much time does an e-mail take to reach us?

It takes just a few seconds! Usually e-mails are delivered instantly (within seconds) to the recipients. But the exact speed of the e-mail depends upon factors, such as Internet traffic and server load at particular times of the day. In general, however, e-mail delivery can be almost instantaneous under best conditions. If you have a good internet speed, you can send an e-mail to a friend halfway around the world, which they will receive within seconds of your sending it!

What is a 3D movie?

A 3D movie refers to a three-dimensional film. Dimensions are extensions in a particular direction. For example, the two-dimensional (2D) images have two dimensions: length and width, while the 3D images have length, width and depth. When you watch a 2D movie, the visual effect is similar to that of a drawing on the paper. In 3D movies, you see a slightly different picture like cars flying towards you or snowflakes floating in the air around you. The 3D effect is experienced in the real world by wearing special glasses which create two different images, so each eye has its own slightly different view. The brain then puts the two images together to form one 3D image that has depth to it.

Find out

What's the difference between 3D and 5D movies?

Pocket fact

First 3D glasses

The first a viewing device that combines 2 pictures in one, a forerunner of the 3D image was invented by William Friese Greene of UK in 1894.

What was the first 3D movie called?

It was called The Power of Love! The first 3D movie shown to an out-of-house audience was The Power of Love, which was premiered at the Ambassador Hotel Theater in Los Angeles on 27 September 1922. This movie used the dual-strip projection and was projected in the red/green anaglyph format. Anaglyph format refers to the 3D effect that is achieved by encoding each eye's image using filters of different colours, typically red and cyan.

What is a mobile network?

A mobile network refers to a radio network distributed over land through cells where each cell includes a fixed location transceiver known as base station. These cells work together to provide radio coverage over larger geographical areas. The network provides services to mobile phone users. These services include making voice and video calls, sending SMS (texts) and MMS messages (picture messages) and internet access.

Pocket fact

The first touchscreen!
The first finger-driven touchscreen was invented by E.A. Johnson in 1965 at the Royal Radar Establishment in Malvern, United Kingdom.

Find out

When was the first mobile phone call made?

What's so special about touchscreens?

It enables the user to interact directly with the display, rather than using a mouse! A touchscreen is an input and output device layered on the top of the electronic visual display of a cell phone or computer. One can give input or control the phone or computer functions through simple or multi-touch gestures by just touching the screen with a special stylus and/or one or more fingers.

When?
.com
@
02:30

When did humans start making stone tools?

Almost 3 million years ago! Stone tools were first made by early humans in East Africa. Early men called *Homo habilis* were the first group of modern humans to make tools. They made different kinds of stone tools like fist-sized hunks of rock and sharp flakes. These tools were known as the Oldowan and used to hunt animals.

Pocket fact

Stone Age!
The time in history when early humans used tools and weapons made out of stone is referred to as Stone Age.

Find out

The Stone Age was divided into three periods. Find their names.

When was iron first used for making tools?

Iron is found in rocks called iron ore. It was discovered by early humans in around 1200 BCE. But the techniques to purify iron and put it to use were first developed in the Middle East after 1500 BCE. Iron could be melted and poured into a mould to make weapons and tools. Iron objects were made by smiths i.e. metal workers.

When were bricks invented?

Bricks were first made around 6,000 years ago. The earliest bricks were made from clay-bearing earth or mud and usually dried in the sun until they were strong enough for use. The oldest discovered bricks date back to around 7500 BC. These were found at Tell Aswad, in the upper Tigris region and in southeast Anatolia close to Diyarbakir.

Pocket fact

The bond!
The patterns created when bricks are laid on the courses are called the bond. To create a durable structure such as fences or houses, the bricks are placed by using mortar. This type of construction is called brickwork.

Find out

When were fruits first grown?

When did humans begin growing crops?

Prior to growing crops, human beings were hunters and gatherers. Farming began around 10,000 BCE. Early men, who had travelled to different places in search of food, began to harvest wild grains they found growing there. They scattered spare grains on the ground to grow more food. Over time, people began to live in settled communities and grew crops on nearby land.

When was the alphabet invented?

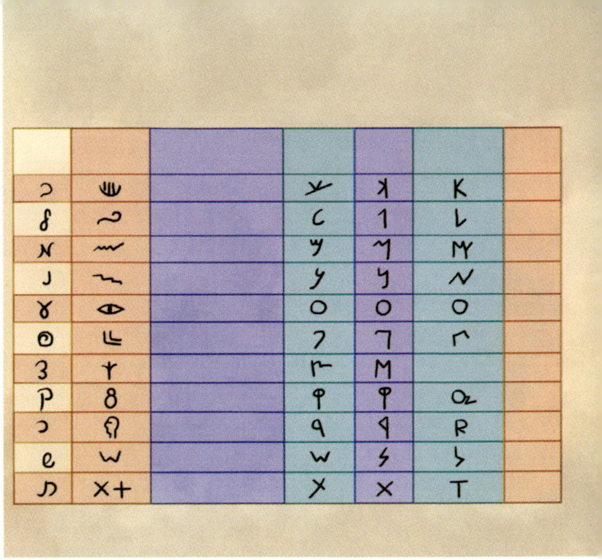

The history of the alphabet started in ancient Egypt in around 2700 BCE. Egyptian writing had a set of some 22 hieroglyphs to represent syllables. But the evolution of modern-day alphabet involved two important steps. The first was the invention of consonantal writing system known as North Semitic by the Phoenicians between 1700 and 1500 BCE. The second was the invention of characters for representing vowels by the Greeks. This happened between 800 and 700 BCE.

Pocket fact

The word *alphabet* comes from the first two letters of the Greek alphabet—alpha and beta.

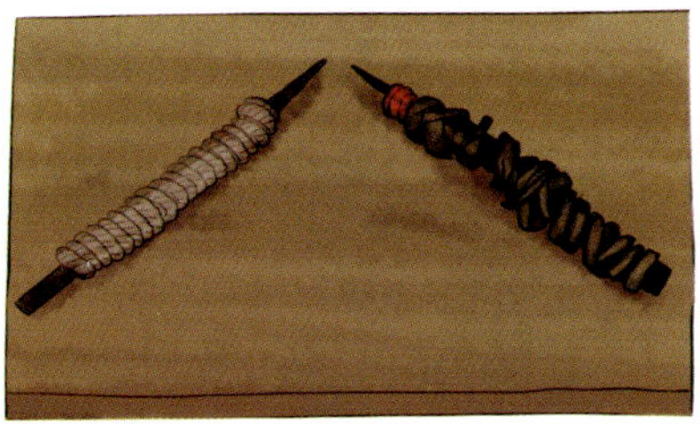

When was the pencil invented?

Find out

When was the eraser invented?

In 1564! Pencils were invented after a large deposit of graphite was found in Borrowdale, England. This new material was brittle but was good for making marks. The graphite ore was cut into large sheets that were then cut into square chunks and fitted into hand-carved wooden holders. The modern pencil was invented by Nicolas-Jacques Conte in 1795.

When was the first ball pen invented?

The ballpoint pen was invented in 1888 by John J. Loud who was attempting to make a writing instrument that could be used for writing on rough surfaces such as wood, coarse wrapping-paper, and other articles. The pen had a small rotating steel ball, held in place by a socket. The pen could be used to mark rough surfaces such as leather but it was very rough for letter-writing.

Pocket fact

The smallest fountain pen!
The 'Nanofountain Probe' is the smallest fountain pen on record. It can write lines that are just 40 nanometre in width.

Find out

What is a stylus? How is it different from a digital pen?

When was the digital pen invented?

A digital pen is an input device which is used to capture the handwriting or brush strokes of a user. It converts handwritten analog information created using "pen and paper" into digital data. This digital data can be utilized in various applications. Digital pens were invented in the early 2000s. They are usually used in conjunction with a digital notebook.

When did Romans invent the first basic concrete?

In the late 3rd century BC! Roman concrete also called opus caementicium was made by adding volcanic dust called pozzolana to mortar made of a mixture of lime or gypsum, brick or rock pieces and water. The concrete was of excellent quality. It was used to build monuments, large buildings, roads and bridges.

Pocket fact

Let's build underwater!
Concrete is one of the only materials used for underwater structures such as dams and submerged bridge piers.

Find out

Which is the largest concrete structure in the world?

When was cement invented?

Cement was invented in 1824 by an English man Joseph Aspdin. He produced it by burning finely ground chalk and clay in a kiln until the carbon dioxide was removed. He called the cement Portland Cement. This is because the concrete made from it looked like high-quality Portland stone, a widely-used building stone in England.

When were the first eyeglasses invented?

Eyeglasses are believed to be invented between 1268 and 1289 in Italy. The earliest eyeglasses were quite different from the ones today. They were just lenses held in front of the eyes or balanced on the nose. Eyeglasses with side or temple pieces that rest over the ear were advertised in 1728 and bifocals were invented by Benjamin Franklin, in 1784.

Find out

What are glasses also known as?

Pocket fact

Reading aid!
The first vision aid was invented around 1000 AD. It was called a reading stone and was created for the far-sighted. It was a glass sphere, and resembled the magnifying glass.

When were contact lenses invented?

The contact lens was invented in 1887 by a Swiss physician A.E. Fick. These lenses were made of glass and were heavy. They also covered the entire eye surface, were difficult to fit and exerted an uncomfortable pressure on the eyeball. Further developments were made when plastic contact lenses were invented in 1938 and the corneal contact lens in 1950.

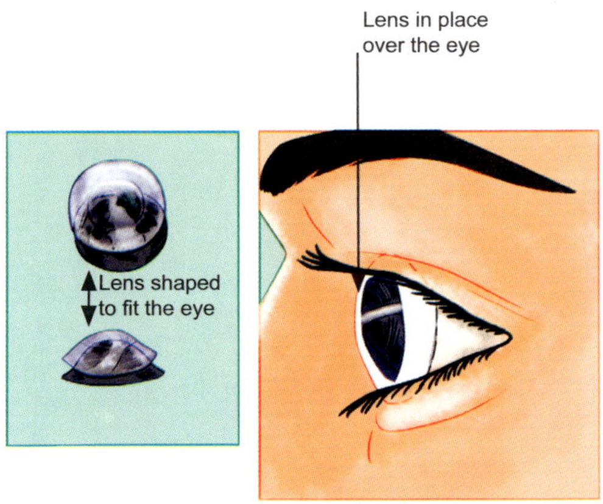

When was the first parachute invented?

Parachutes had been imagined and sketched by Abbas Ibn Firnas and Leonardo Da Vinci before its invention. In 1595, the Croatian inventor Faust Vrančić designed a parachute-like device. But the first modern parachute was invented by Sebastien Lenormand in 1783. It is believed that he mounted the tower of the Montpellier Observatory in France and jumped with a 14-foot (4.3-metre) parachute, landing unharmed.

Find out

What are present day hot air balloons made up of?

Pocket fact

Flying man!
The early parachute design was called "Homo Volans" which means Flying Man.

When was hot air balloon invented?

In the late 1700s! In 1766, Henry Cavendish proposed the idea that objects can be lifted from Earth using hydrogen. This idea was taken a step further by Joseph Michel Montgolfier from France in 1782. He used a silk bag filled with hot air and made it rise and fly for 10 minutes. Michael and his brother Jacques-Etienne worked further and in September, 1783 they made a balloon using a large spherical bag filled with hot air. This eventually led to the invention of modern hot air balloons.

When was the mercury thermometer invented?

In 1714! The mercury thermometer with a standardized scale, was invented by the German physicist Daniel Gabriel Fahrenheit. It was made of a bulb containing mercury attached to a glass tube of narrow diameter. In 1724, Daniel also introduced the standard temperature scale_Fahrenheit Scale_that was used to record changes in temperature.

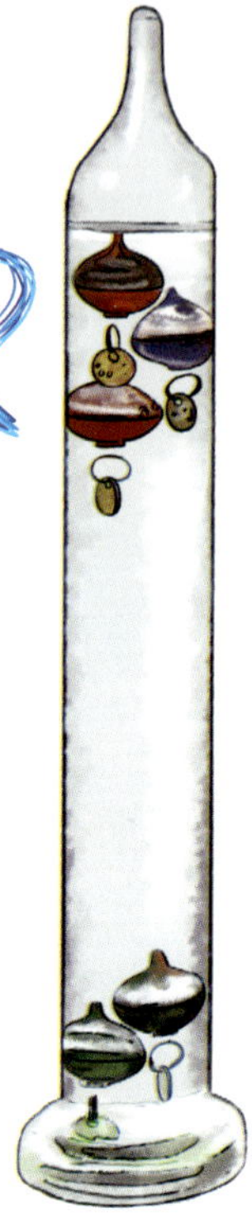

Pocket fact

I named it!
The credit for naming the barometer goes to an Englishman named Robert Boyle. He took the name from two Greek words baros and meter in 1665. The meaning of these words is measuring weight.

Find out

What are the three major temperature scales for use in the thermometer?

When was the barometer invented?

In the mid-17th century! A barometer is a device used to measure atmospheric pressure. The mercury barometer is the oldest type of barometer. It was invented by the Italian physicist Evangelista Torricelli in 1643. It was made using a 10-m long glass tube filled with water. But this was quite inconvenient so Torricelli reconstructed it using a four-foot long glass tube filled with mercury inverted into a dish of mercury. The level of mercury dropped and rose according to the atmospheric pressure.

When were microphones invented?

The first microphone was invented in 1877. It was called a carbon microphone and composed of two electrical contacts separated by a thin layer of carbon. One contact was attached to a diaphragm that vibrated when struck by a sound wave. The other was connected to the output. It was the first microphone that enabled proper voice telephony.

Find out

Which scientist was greatly helped by the speech synthesizer?

Pocket fact

Microphones were used initially for talking on the telephone as radio transmitters. As transmitters they were used to help pass on waves carrying messages or signals.

When was the first speech synthesizer invented?

In the late 1700s! The first speech synthesizer was invented by Wolfgang von Kempelen. It consisted of a pressure chamber for the lungs, a vibrating reed that acted as vocal cords, and a leather tube for the vocal tract action. It produced different vowel sounds by manipulating the shape of the leather tube and consonant sounds were simulated by four separate constricted passages. Later in 1800s, Charles Wheatstone constructed his famous version of von Kempelen's speaking machine.

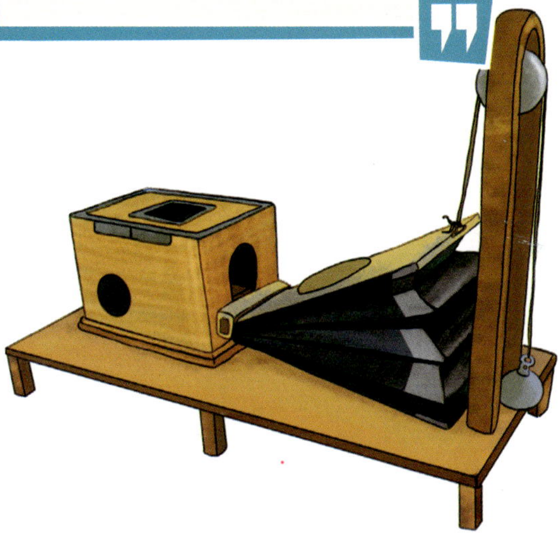

When was sound first recorded and played back on metal foil?

The phonograph was the first device that was used for recording and reproducing sound mechanically. It was invented by Thomas Edison in 1877. It had a thin sheet of tin foil wrapped around a hand-cranked, grooved, metal cylinder. It could play back sound by reading hollow cylinders that had the audio recording impressed on the outside surface. Later, wax was used as the recording medium for engraving instead of tin foil and came to be known as the Edison wax cylinder.

Find out

What is the full form of mp3?

Pocket fact

From Greek words!
The term 'phonograph' comes from two Greek words translated phonē and graphē meaning 'sound' and 'writing' respectively.

When was the digital audio player invented?

It was invented in 1979. The first portable digital audio player called the IXI was designed by British inventor Ken Kramer. It had a memory chip that could only store a few minutes of uncompressed audio. The high performance audio compression method later known as MP3 was developed between the late 1980s and early 1990s.

When was the first electric washing machine invented?

The first electric washing machine was introduced in 1908 by the Hurley Machine Company of Chicago, Illinois. It was invented by Alva J. Fisher and called the Thor. It resembled a drum with a galvanized tub and an electric motor. It had a series of blades that lifted the clothes as the cylinder rotated. After 8 rotations in one direction, the machine would reverse rotation so that the clothes did not wad up into a compact mass.

Find out

How much water does a dishwasher use in one cycle?

Pocket fact

No change!
Modern day washing machine was invented in 1908, and amazingly its design has not changed much in last 100 years.

When was the dishwasher invented?

The first practical dishwashing machine was invented in 1886 by Josephine Cochran. It was a hand operated machine with wire compartments to hold dishes which were sprayed with hot soapy water. It had a wheel that was turned using a hand crank on the outside the machine. This dishwasher was initially bought only by hotels and large restaurants. It was sold to the general public after the 1950s.

When was the first smartphone invented?

The term smartphone was used by people in around 1995, but the first true smartphone was invented by IBM in 1992. It was called the Simon Personal Communicator. Apart from its calling features, the smartphone had a monochrome LCD touchscreen measuring 4.5 inches by 1.4 inches, and it came with a stylus. It could be used to send and receive emails, faxes, and pages.

Pocket fact

The toughest!
Sonim XP3300 Force is recognized as the toughest phone by Guinness World Records. It was dropped from 84ft and survived without any operational damage.

Find out

What is an e-book?

When was the first automated reader invented?

The world's first automated reader was invented by a school teacher Angela Ruiz Robles in Spain, 1949. She wanted to create a reader that would be far easier to carry for school children, than a number of different text books. This automated reader had a smaller amount of text printed onto spools and was operated by compressed air. This book was not electronic, yet it is hailed as the first automated reader.

When was the supercomputer invented?

The supercomputer was created in 1964 by an electrical engineer Seymour Cray. Known as the CDC 6600, the supercomputer ran at a speed of 40 MHz and executed roughly three million floating-point operations per second. This made it the fastest computer in the world. Often considered to be the world's first supercomputer, the CDC 6600 was 10 times faster than most computers.

Pocket fact

So many jobs!
Supercomputers can do arithmetic jobs very fast. Hence they are used for code-breaking, weather forecasting, genetic analysis and other jobs that need many calculations.

Find out

Who invented the Internet?

When does the Internet face traffic?

The Internet is a global network connecting millions of computers worldwide. More than 190 countries are linked to one another and can share data and information. Internet traffic is the term used to describe the flow of data across the Internet. It happens when a lot of data is shared and received at the same time.

Why?

Why was the number zero invented?

The number zero was invented independently by the Indians and the Mayans. Before the invention of zero, people used an empty space to indicate its value. This was confusing because an empty space was also used as a separator between numbers. To avoid confusion, people started using a dot to represent zero, which eventually took the form of the number zero that we use today.

Pocket fact

The arithmometer!

The arithmometer was the first commercially successful calculating machine. It could perform all four basic operations — addition, subtraction, multiplication and division. It was invented by Charles Xavier Thomas de Colmar in 1820.

Find out

What happens when you divide a number by zero?

Why are the numbers on a calculator reversed?

Research indicates that zero is the most commonly used number in numerical calculations. Pressing it repeatedly would not be convenient if it was placed in the middle of the number pad, and it would invariably result in errors. This is the reason zero is kept at the bottom of the calculator and the numbers 1, 2 and 3 are placed near it.

Why did the earliest forks have only two tines?

They were not used for dining! Forks were invented in Europe, thousands of years ago. The earlier forks had only two tines. These forks were used as agricultural and kitchen tools. Later on, people started using forks to eat food. However, this became a problem because diners often accidentally injured themselves with it. To solve this problem, the number of tines on the forks was increased. Nowadays, forks with four tines are considered most comfortable for use by diners.

> **Pocket fact**
>
> **Not just a pinch of salt!**
>
> Salt is used as a food preservative because bacteria cannot grow in salty conditions. Salt was used as an effective preservative even in the ancient times and this made it a precious commodity back in the day.

> **Find out**
>
> What is cutlery?

Why were food preservatives invented?

To preserve food for longer durations and prevent it from getting spoiled! Food preservation is said to have enabled ancient people to settle down and form a community. The ancient preservation methods included salting, fermentation, oil packing, pickling and smoking. The technique of canning food was discovered in the 19th century by Nicholas Apert.

Why were stickers invented?

For advertisement and for use as postage stamps and tax stamps! A sticker refers to an adhesive label. The exact information about the invention of stickers remains unknown. It is said that they were first used by Egyptians to advertise their daily market rates. They were also used as postage stamps and tax stamps. R. Stanton Avery is said to have invented the first self-adhesive label in the 1930s.

Pocket fact

Bumper Stickers!
Bumper stickers were invented by a printer named Forest Gill. They were made for advertising Rocky Mountain's Rock City attraction.

Find out

Where has the word pencil been derived from?

Why is pencil lead called lead?

As graphite was mistaken for lead! Pencil lead is made of graphite. When graphite was first discovered in England in the form of a large solid black mass, it was thought to be black lead. People used sticks of graphite for marking. The sticks were so brittle that they could be used only after they were wrapped in sheep skin or put into hollowed-out wood sticks. This led to the invention of pencil. And till date the inner marking portion of a pencil is referred to as lead.

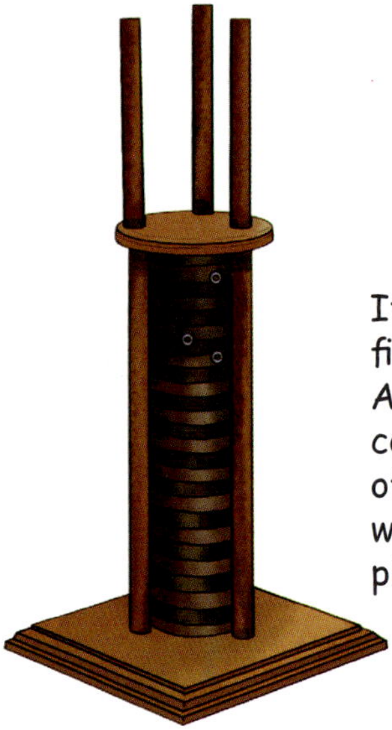

Why was the first battery called the voltaic pile?

It was named after its inventor! Voltaic pile is the first ever battery invented by the Italian scientist Alessandro Volta. It was a pile of discs made from copper and zinc. Each pile was separated by a piece of leather or cardboard soaked in weak acid or salt water. Volta found that electricity flowed through the pile of discs and hence called it the voltaic pile.

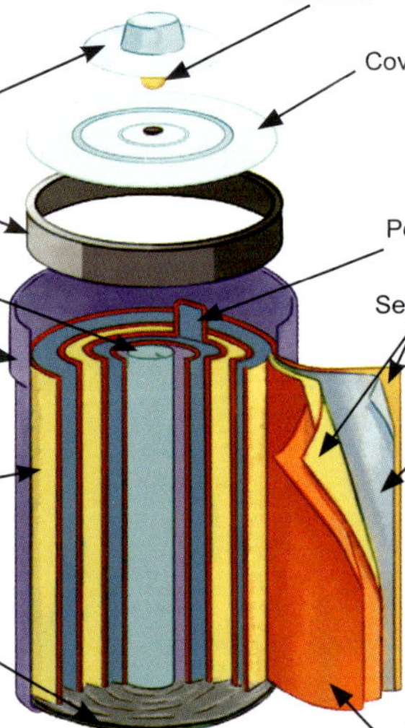

Pocket fact

Benjamin Franklin was the first to use the word "battery" in 1748. He used it in reference to Leyden jars. This word was borrowed from the military terminology.

Why is nickel so popular in batteries?

These batteries have a longer shelf life! Nickel is a metal that is widely used in batteries. Nickel-based batteries last longer as compared to the other batteries. They can be stored in a discharged state and can be transported easily. Also, nickel-based batteries can be recharged very quickly. These are low cost batteries and are available in a wide range of sizes.

Try this!

When was the first rechargeable battery invented?

Why did the first vacuum cleaners have wooden handles?

To move the bellows! The first vacuum cleaner was invented in the 1860s. It consisted of bellows that sucked dirt into the vacuum cleaner. It also had a wooden handle, which was moved back and forth to create vacuum in the tube to suck up dust. It was much later that electrically operated vacuum cleaners were invented.

Find out

Name the first robotic vacuum cleaner.

Pocket fact

The inspiration!
H.C. Booth got his inspiration to invent the vacuum cleaner while travelling on a train. He put a handkerchief across his mouth and sucked up as much dust into it as he could. The vacuum filter was invented shortly after.

Why wasn't the first electric vacuum cleaner successful?

Due to its complexity! The first electric vacuum cleaner was invented by Hubert Cecil Booth in 1901. It was in the form of a large, horse-drawn, petrol-driven unit. It blasted out the dust and blew it with compressed air into a receptacle; the dust was not sucked into the unit. These vacuum cleaners were not very portable.

Why were the first bicycles called boneshakers?

They juddered over every bump and road! Bicycles were first invented in 1817 by the German nobleman Baron von Drais. These bicycles were made of wooden frames and iron wheels.

They lacked pedals. The first pedal-driven bicycle was invented by Pierre Lallement in 1864. It had pedals and cranks on the front wheel to give simultaneous balance and power. These bicycles juddered over every bump and road; and hence they were called "boneshakers".

Try this!

Can you name all the parts of a bicycle? Give it a try!

Pocket fact

Let's race!

One of the most famous bicycle races in the world is the Tour de France. It was established in 1903 and is considered to be the ultimate test of endurance.

Why were bicycle gears invented?

To make cycling easy! In the 1800s, bicyclists had a difficult time while cycling on hilly roads, as it was tough to pedal. In 1871, James Starley invented the Ariel which was probably the first geared bike. Bicycles with gears were invented so that bicyclists could pedal comfortably on any terrain. They could shift to an easier gear on upside roads or when riding into the wind. These gears do all the hard work of moving the chain from one sprocket (chain ring) to the next!

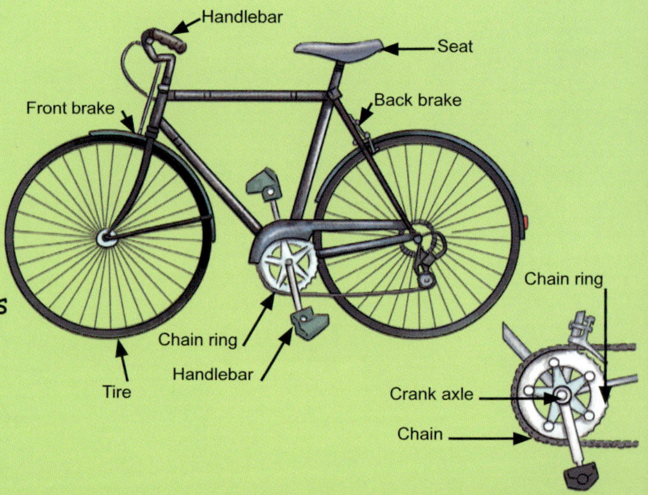

Why were Ford's Model T cars black?

Since black paint dried fast! Henry Ford's Model T car was first sold in 1908. It was sturdy, reliable and easy to drive. It became the first car to be mass-produced in 1913, with almost 10,000 cars manufactured each day. From 1914 to 1925, all the Model T cars manufactured were black in colour because black paint dried the quickest. This allowed the assembly line to operate at top speed and manufacture more cars!

Find out

How much time does it take to change a Volkswagen Beetle's engine?

Pocket fact

The first Model T cars were sold for around $850! But their price fell to $260 by 1925.

Why was Volkswagen's Beetle named so?

Due to its bug-like shape! VW Beetle is one of the most popular cars manufactured by the Volkswagen Group. It is also known as the people's car. The Beetle got its name from its downward-pointing front and curved back, which give it a bug-like shape. This streamlined shape reduces air resistance, resulting in lesser fuel consumption.

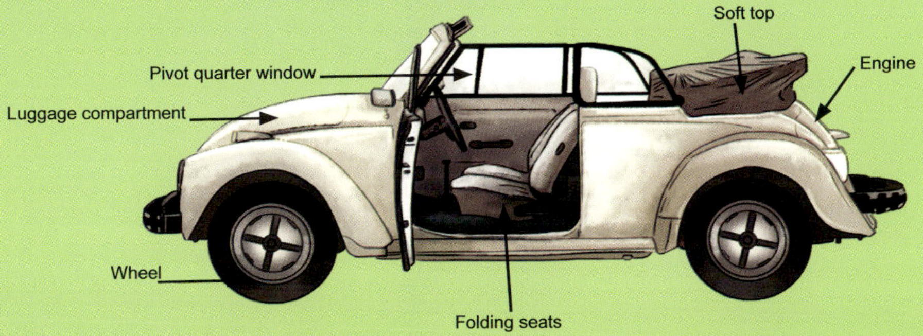

Why were oil-based inks invented?

So that they don't blur when used in the press! Many ancient cultures around the world discovered and invented different kinds of ink. In the ancient times, natural plants (plant dyes) or graphite ground with water were used as ink. But they tended to blur when used in printing. It was Gutenberg who developed an oil-based ink in the 15th century. It was made from soot, turpentine, walnut oil and unknown plant extracts. This ink was more resilient than water-based inks.

Find out

What are modern-day inks made of?

Pocket fact

Roots of 3D printing!
In 1984, Chuck Hull invented a process called "stereolithography". In this process, UV lasers were used to solidify photopolymers that created 3D parts layer by layer.

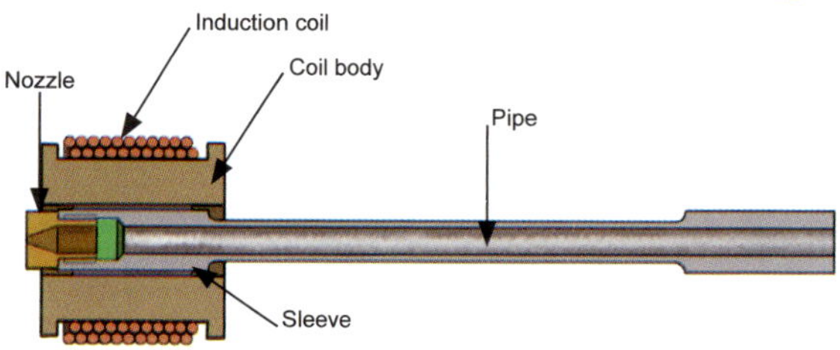

Why do 3D printers have heating elements?

To melt plastic! A 3D printer is a device that creates a three-dimensional model of an object. Many 3D printers have a heating element. This heating element is used to melt the material that is used in printing. The molten material is passed through a steel pipe to a nozzle. The layers of this material are shaped into the desired object, which solidifies quickly after coming out of the printer.

Why were windmills a common sight in olden days?

They were used to pump water and for many other works! Windmills are used to generate energy which can be used in many ways. In olden days, windmills made work easier. They were used for pumping water, grinding grains and spices and sawing wood. They were a common sight in agricultural fields prior to the invention of modern agricultural implements.

Find out

Which one of these produces electricity—wind turbines or wind mills?

Pocket fact

That's tall!
The largest wind turbine in the world is located in Hawaii. It is 20-storey tall and has blades the length of a football field.

Why don't we use waterwheels anymore?

Waterwheel is a huge wheel driven by flowing water. When water is flowed over it, it moves. In olden days, the energy produced from waterwheels was used for different purposes such as milling flour, grinding wood, or pounding fibre for cloth making and so on. But these machines were dependent on flowing water. They could be located only near flowing water bodies. So they were replaced by smaller, less expensive turbines, which generated hydroelectricity.

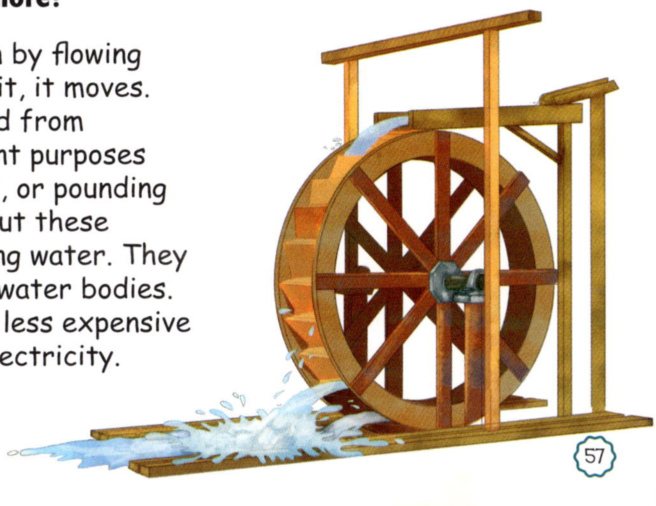

Why was camera obscura called a dark room?

In the ancient times when there were no cameras, the principle of camera obscura was used to reflect images. In Latin "camera" means room and "obscura" means dark, hence the name "dark room". It refers to a dark room with a small hole in one wall. On the wall opposite to the hole, an upside-down image of the object outside is formed. This was first recorded by the Chinese philosopher Mo-Ti in the 5th century BC. He called this darkened room a "collecting place" or the "locked treasure room".

Try this

Use the principle of "camera obscura" and make a pinhole camera with the help of your parents.

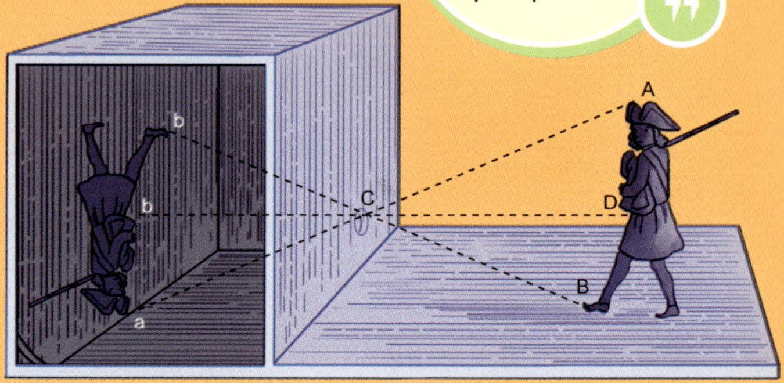

Pocket fact

Say cheese!

Clicking photographs wasn't always as simple as the "smile and click" routine we follow today. Early cameras were so slow that it would take several hours to actually capture a film!

Why did camera reels go out of fashion?

They were replaced by digital cameras! The first cameras used reels that were developed into photographs. However, with the invention of the digital camera, people stopped using cameras with reels. The reason behind this was the easy distribution, easy transport, low cost and high clarity of the photographs taken with digital cameras. Also, reels can get spoilt due to scratches and tears but digital photographs retain their quality for a much longer duration.

Why were notes and coins invented?

To make buying and selling fair and easier! In the ancient times, people used barter system as a means of exchange. Over time, this system created problems for people. Like, wheat could be exchanged only when harvested, fruit only when ripened and that too before it got spoiled. Such issues with the commodities led people to create coins out of precious metals to use as money.

Find out

What are the two sides of a coin called?

Pocket fact

On the coin!
Romans were the first to stamp the image of a living person on a coin. They used Julius Caesar's image on a coin in 44 BCE.

Why do debit cards have chips?

To make them more secure! Debit cards are made with a magnetic strip, which comprises all the information about an individual's bank account. To prevent the misuse of these cards, a chip was introduced. While the magnetic strip has the unchanging data of a person's bank account, the chip creates unique codes every time the card is used. So it's almost impossible to duplicate it.

Why do Braille cells have six dots?

So that they can fit on a fingertip! Braille is a system of reading and writing used by the visually impaired. It was invented by Louis Braille. Its characters are represented by patterns of raised dots that can be felt with the fingertips. Each Braille cell consists of six dots that are arranged in different patterns to make up letters of the alphabet, numbers and punctuation marks. The size, shape and positions of the "Braille cell" were created by Louis Braille. Four dots did not give enough variations in dot placement, while eight dots were too large for a fingertip. So, the classic arrangement came to be six dots.

Pocket fact

Without a name!

Great Britain is the only country that prints stamps without its name on them. It was they who invented stamps!

Why were stamps invented?

To recover the cost of the mail! Before the invention of stamps, the person who received a mail had to pay for it. However, if the recipient was not available, or was unable or unwilling to pay for the mail, the cost of the mail was not recovered. To overcome this problem, postage stamps were invented. These stamps indicated that the mail bearing them had been paid for. The first-issued postage stamp called the British Penny Black Stamp was released in Great Britain in 1840.

Find out

When is the World Braille Day celebrated?

Why were video games invented?

To increase TV sales! The first video game was invented after an engineer named Ralph H. Baer created the prototype for the world's first video game console. Baer worked for a television manufacturer. He came up with the idea to incorporate an electronic video game into a TV set to increase sales. The company rejected his plan, but Baer eventually developed a prototype console in 1967. This became the world's first video game console called Magnavox Odyssey.

Find out

Why are mobile apps named so?

Pocket fact

CD technology!
The 3DO was the first video game system that was based entirely on CD technology. It was introduced in 1993.

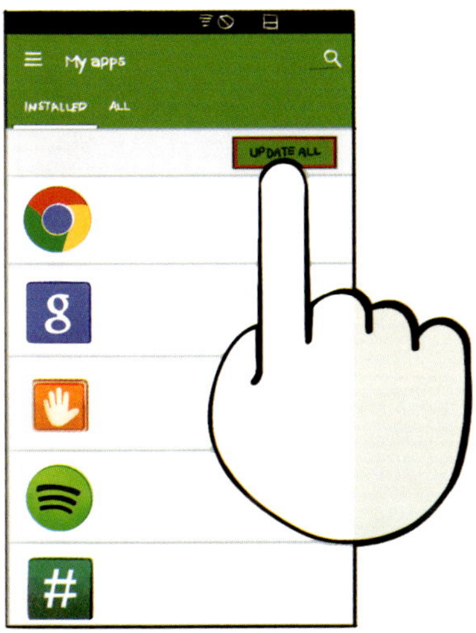

Why do we need to update apps?

To update their security! You must have often noticed the "update your app" notification on your mobile phone and computer. This indicates that the app you are using has been enhanced with new and improved features. By updating the app, you can ensure that your phone and computer are up-to-date and secure. When an app is updated, it fixes the existing bugs in the software. Major companies regularly update their apps because they want to fix the flaws in their app before hackers try to misuse them.

Index

OTHER TITLES IN THIS SERIES